KALEIDOSCOPE

THE PRESIDENT

by
Suzanne LeVert

BENCHMARK BOOKS

MARSHALL CAVENDISH
NEW YORK

Benchmark Books
Marshall Cavendish Corporation
99 White Plains Road
Tarrytown, NY 10591-9001
www.marshallcavendish.com

LeVert, Suzanne.
        The president / by Suzanne LeVert.
p.cm. – (Kaleidoscope)
Includes bibliographical references and index.
Contents: The office of the president – The presidency through time – What it takes – Becoming president.
ISBN 0-7614-1454-1
1. Presidents—United States—Juvenile literature. [1. Presidents.] I. Title. II. Kaleidoscope (Tarrytown, N.Y.)
I. Title. II. Kaleidoscope (Tarrytown, N.Y.)
JK517 .L48 2003
352.23'0973—dc21

                                            2002000066

Photo Research by Anne Burns Images

Cover Photo: Corbis/Joseph Sohm; Visions of America

Photographs in this book are used by permission and through the courtesy of:

North Wind Pictures: 4; *Corbis*:10, 21, 30; p.6 Adam Woolfitt; 22 Paul Almasy; 29 AFP; 38 Bettman; 41; Reuters NewMedia Inc.
Superstock: 9; *Liaison*:13, 37 Mark Wilson/Newsmakers;17 Pool Photo/Newsmakers;18 Hulton; 33 David McNew/Newsmakers; 34
Joe Raedle/Newsmakers; 25 Hulton; *Art Resource*, NY:14 The Andy Warhol Foundation; *Nixon Library*:26

Printed in Italy

6 5 4 3 2 1

CONTENTS

THE OFFICE OF THE PRESIDENT

"I do solemnly swear that I will faithfully execute the office of president of the United States, and will, to the best of my ability, preserve, protect, and defend the Constitution of the United States."

Every four years since 1789, when George Washington became our nation's first president, a man has taken that solemn oath. As the head of one of the world's wealthiest and most powerful nations, the president plays a crucial leadership role both at home and abroad.

George Washington, the first president of the United States, was inaugurated on April 30, 1789. He took the oath of office from the balcony of Federal Hall in New York City.

5

Written in 1787, the Constitution of the United States established our country's *federal*, or national, government. It created three separate branches of government: the *judicial* branch (the Supreme Court) to interpret the law, the *legislative* branch (Congress) to enact the law, and the *executive* branch (the president) to enforce the law. The president of the United States is the head of the executive branch. It is his responsibility to report the state of the nation to Congress every year and to suggest that Congress put into effect, or enact, any laws that he feels are necessary. The president is the country's most visible foreign representative, working with other world leaders on economic, social, and other *policies*. He is also the chief defender of the rights described in the United States Constitution.

The Supreme Court is the highest court of the judicial branch of the United States government. It decides cases in the Supreme Court Building, located in Washington, D.C.

The Constitution gives the president wide powers, but it balances that power with the Supreme Court and the Congress. For instance, as commander in chief of the armed forces, the president is responsible for national defense. Yet only Congress has the power to declare war.

On September 17, 1789, thirty-nine of the fifty-five delegates to the Constitutional Convention signed the final draft of the United States Constitution. This document remains the oldest and the shortest written constitution of any government in the world.

The president may have strong ideas about what policies the country should follow, but only Congress can turn those policies into laws, and only the Supreme Court can judge whether those laws are constitutional—or, are in keeping with the Constitution. Nevertheless, the president remains one of the most important elected officials in the world, helping to shape events and issues both at home and abroad.

But the president does not perform the duties of the executive office alone. He receives advice and information from members of his *cabinet* and from representatives of other government agencies. The president also has a large personal staff to assist him in his daily activities.

Although his office is a civilian one, the U.S. president serves as commander in chief of the armed services. Here, former president Ronald Regan inspects the troops.

STANDING READY: THE VICE PRESIDENT

One of the most important members of the executive branch is the *vice president*. Only a heartbeat away from being the most powerful elected official in the world, the vice president must be ready to become president or acting president in an instant if the president becomes unable to perform the duties of office for any reason. In addition to his other duties and responsibilities, the vice president also serves as the head officer of the United States Senate and has the title of president of the Senate.

Vice President Dick Cheney was inaugurated to serve under President George W. Bush on January 20, 2001.

14

STANDING ALONGSIDE: THE FIRST LADY

The president's wife is called the *first lady*. First ladies serve important roles. Some have concentrated on social activities in the White House—which is where the president and his family resides—such as receptions and dinners. Others have taken on much larger responsibilities. Abigail Adams, wife of the second president, John Adams, promoted women's rights. In 1919, Edith Wilson helped run President Woodrow Wilson's administration when he became ill.

One of the most glamorous first ladies, Jacqueline Bouvier Kennedy, wife of John F. Kennedy, Jr., served as first lady from 1961 to 1963, when her husband was assassinated.

Eleanor Roosevelt spoke out on issues of social welfare during and after the presidency of her husband, Franklin Delano Roosevelt. From 1993 to 2001, Hillary Rodham Clinton worked behind the scenes on such vital concerns as health care reform and children's rights when her husband, Bill Clinton, was president. She now serves as one of New York's U.S. senators.

Hillary Rodham Clinton was one of the most publicly outspoken and politically active first ladies.

THE PRESIDENCY THROUGH TIME

The people of the newly formed United States of America chose George Washington to be their first president. He served as president for eight years, from 1789 to 1797. Our third president, Thomas Jefferson, expanded his power when he entered into a treaty with France called the Louisiana Purchase. Before the Louisiana Purchase, the United States was quite small. After the treaty, the country nearly doubled in size. The sixteenth president, Abraham Lincoln, further increased presidential power when he took certain military actions during the Civil War, such as blockading Southern ports. Although he used powers the

Abraham Lincoln served as president of the United States during the Civil War, when the country was divided.

19

Constitution reserved for Congress, his leadership helped preserve the country during a social and military crisis.

The United States became a world power—and the president a world leader—during the late 1800s and early 1900s. In 1898, President William McKinley led the nation to victory over Spain in the Spanish-American War. In this way, the United States fought to free the island of Cuba from Spanish rule. Then, in 1917, President Woodrow Wilson raised support for entering World War I among Americans, to "make the world safe for democracy." World War I was a military struggle for power and territory, and included nearly twenty-five nations, mostly on the European continent.

Survivors of the American battleship Maine, destroyed by a Spanish mine in the harbor of Havana, Cuba, in 1898. The sinking of the Maine triggered the Spanish-American War.

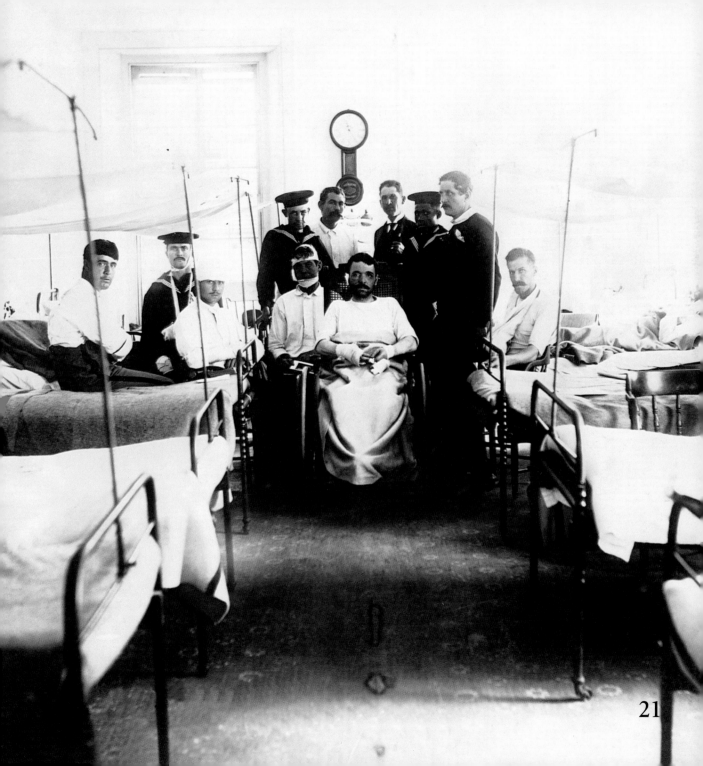

21

22

After the war, President Wilson played a major role in establishing the *League of Nations*, an international organization dedicated to maintaining peace. Although the United States never joined the League, Wilson received the Nobel Peace Prize for his efforts. The League of Nations formed the model for the United Nations, established in 1945.

Founded on October 24, 1945, the United Nations is located in New York City. However, the land and the buildings on it are international territory, and the United Nations has its own flag, post office, and postage stamps.

During the 1930s and early 1940s, President Franklin Delano Roosevelt guided the country through the crisis of the *Great Depression*, a period when millions of Americans lost their jobs and their homes. Working closely with Congress, he helped to create programs and reforms, called the New Deal, that created jobs and offered support for families. He also led the country as it fought against Germany, Japan, and their allies in World War II, during the first half of the 1940s. During the administrations of Harry Truman and Dwight Eisenhower, the United States solidified its position as a world leader. Under their leadership, the country's economy became the richest and its military forces one of the most respected in the world.

Franklin Delano Roosevelt, president for more than twelve years, led the country during the Great Depression. He was the only president to be elected to four terms. After his death, Congress enacted the Twenty-second Amendment to the Constitution, which limits the time a president can serve to two terms.

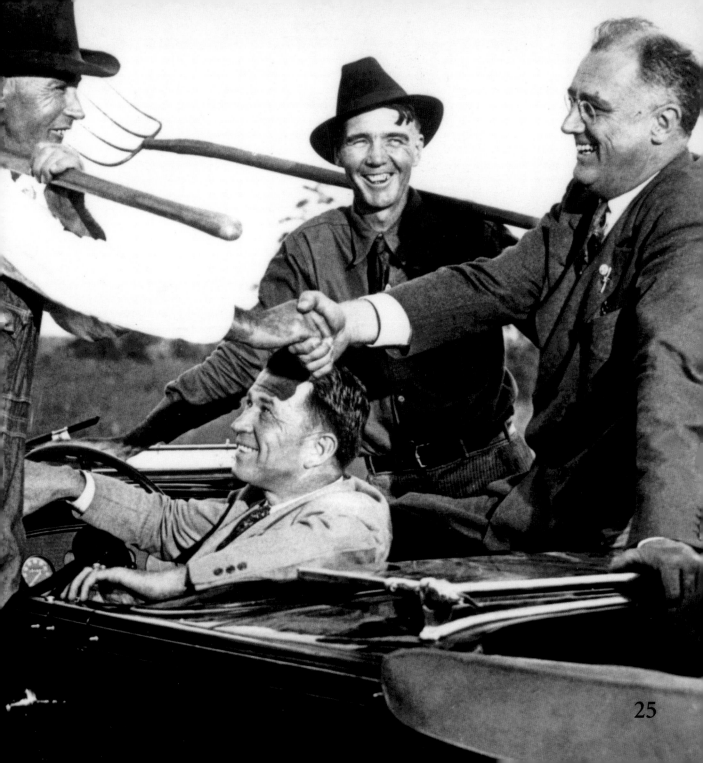

26

However, the presidency suffered when the United States became involved in the Vietnam War. During the 1960s and early 1970s, President Lyndon Johnson and his successor, President Richard Nixon, sent nearly nine million U.S. troops to support South Vietnam in its war against communist North Vietnam. Many Americans opposed the nation's participation in the war and felt that both Johnson and Nixon had usurped, or taken control of, Congress's power and misled the country about the nation's activities in the war.

Richard Milhous Nixon, president of the United States from 1969 until he resigned the office in 1974, remains one of the country's most controversial leaders.

Since the Vietnam War, the president and Congress have involved the U.S. military in several actions, including the Persian Gulf War in 1991. The world considers the United States to be one of the greatest military powers and looks to the president as the leader of the free world. At the same time, the president's role as chief executive at home has continued to grow as well. Millions of Americans look to the president for leadership on issues such as education, health care, and other economic and social issues.

Bill Clinton served the United States as president from 1993 to 2001. Although his administration was marked by personal scandal, the country experienced great economic growth and prosperity during those years.

WHAT IT TAKES: BECOMING PRESIDENT

There are three requirements all presidents must meet. First, they must be born American citizens. Second, they must be at least thirty-five years old. Third, they must have lived in the United States for at least fourteen years. Although only white males have been elected president so far, the office is open to women and minorities.

Presidential elections take place every four years in the United States. Election Day is always the first Tuesday in November, but the *campaign* starts long

Elected president at the age of forty-three in 1960, John F. Kennedy became one of the most admired presidents in U.S. history. While campaigning for his second term, Kennedy was shot to death by an assassin in Dallas, Texas, on November 22, 1963.

before that. Four months before the election, the major political parties—the Democrats and Republicans— hold *conventions* to choose their presidential candidates.

Then these candidates–their parties' official nominees—face weeks of hard work on the campaign trail, giving speeches, *debating*, and bringing their views to as many Americans as possible.

On Election Day, all adult American citizens, except those convicted of felony crimes, are eligible to vote. People vote at polling places, which are set up in schools, libraries, and other public buildings. When all the votes cast by U.S. citizens are counted, the result is called the *popular vote*. In most cases, the winner of the popular vote becomes president, but not always. That depends on the vote of the *electoral college*.

Democratic Party convention–goers celebrate Al Gore's presidential nomination on August 17, 2000.

The electoral college is a group of people called electors. Their job is to cast a vote according to the will of the state they represent. The number of electors from each state is equal to the number of senators and members of the House of Representatives from that state. To win the national election, a presidential candidate must receive 270 out of the 538 electoral votes—no matter how many popular votes he or she receives.

The right to vote is one of the most precious of the rights provided to the American people by the United States Constitution. Here, residents of El Paso, Texas, cast their ballot for president of the United States.

In the election of 2000, for instance, Republican George W. Bush and his running mate, Dick Cheney, earned a total of 271 electoral votes. Even though Democrat Al Gore and his running mate, Joseph Lieberman, won about 540,000 more popular votes, Bush and Cheney won the election. It took almost six weeks to confirm these results. But on January 20, 2001, George W. Bush took the oath of office to become the forty-third president of the United States. The fact that the nation remained stable during the long contest showed the world just how strong our democracy and the office of the presidency of the United States really is.

Flanked by members of his family and Vice President Dick Cheney, George W. Bush takes the oath of the office of president from Supreme Court Chief Justice William Rehnquist on January 20, 2001.

BECOMING PRESIDENT

The president is *inaugurated*, or sworn in, to office on January 20 following the election. Thousands of people watch the ceremony, which always takes place at noon outside the Capitol building in Washington, D.C. A president serves a term of four years. He can be reelected for a second term, for a total of eight years. A president may not run again if he has served two terms.

The United States Capitol building is home to both houses of Congress. The Supreme Court and the Library of Congress, among other government buildings, are located within the Capitol complex.

Today the presidency remains a strong and vital office. As countries around the world become increasingly dependent economically and culturally on one another, the president's role as a world leader is an important one. Americans continue to look to the president for leadership and morale. Most important, the president still serves as the prime defender of the United States Constitution.

President George W. Bush motivates firefighters and rescue workers to continue their hard work at the site of the World Trade Center terrorist attacks of September 11, 2001.

GLOSSARY

Cabinet A group of government officials who head departments in the executive branch and advise the president.

Convention The speeches, rallies, fund-raising events, and other events designed to win votes for two or more candidates who want to be elected to a certain office.

Debate A formal meeting between two or more candidates designed to contrast their views about the issues facing the American public.

Electoral college A group of representatives chosen by voters of each state to elect the president and vice president.

Executive branch The branch of government responsible for enforcing the law. The executive branch consists of the president, vice president, the cabinet, and other agencies.

Federal The central, national level of government, formed by agreement among the states. The states retain certain independent powers, but the federal government acts in the nation's name in areas such as national defense and foreign affairs.

First lady The president's wife.

Great Depression A period of economic decline in the United States and around the world during the 1930s and early 1940s. Vast numbers of people were out of work, prices of agricultural and other products fell dramatically, and banks and other financial institutions failed.

Inaugurate To officially invest a newly elected president with the powers and responsibilities of the office of the presidency.

Judicial branch The federal courts, including the Supreme Court, responsible for interpreting the laws.

League of Nations An international association established in 1919 to maintain peace after World War I. The League of Nations dispersed during World War II, but was the model for the United Nations.

Legislation The process of passing laws.

Legislative branch The branch of government responsible for creating and enacting laws, made up of the two houses of Congress; the House of Representatives and the Senate.

Policy A program carried out or proposed by a member of government or of a government agency.

Popular vote The total number of the general public who vote for president and vice president during a presidential election.

Vice president The person who serves directly under the president in the executive branch. The vice president serves as the president of the United States Senate and must be ready to act as president if the president becomes ill or dies while in office.

FIND OUT MORE

BOOKS

Kessler, Paula N. and Justin Segal. *The President's Almanac*. Chicago: Lowell House, 1996.

Quiri, Patricia Ryon. *Congress*. New York: Children's Press, 1998.

Sobel, Syl. *Presidential Elections and Other Cool Facts*. Hauppague, NY: Barron's Educational Series, 2000

Spies, Karen. *Our Presidency*. Brookfield, CT: The Millbrook Press, 1994.

WEB SITES

www.theamericanpresidency.net

www.whitehouse.gov

www.firstgov.gov

AUTHOR'S BIO

Suzanne LeVert is the author of nearly a dozen books for young readers on a host of different topics, including biographies of former governor of Louisiana Huey Long and author Edgar Allan Poe. Most recently, she wrote four books in Benchmark Books' Kaleidoscope series on the human body, *The Brain*, *The Heart*, *The Lungs,* and *Bones And Muscles*.

INDEX

Page numbers for illustrations are in boldface.